BROKEN GLASS AND GASOLINE

BY SOKRATIS J IVANOVICH

DORRANCE
PUBLISHING CO
EST. 1920
PITTSBURGH, PENNSYLVANIA 15238

Dorrance Publishing Co
585 Alpha Drive
Suite 103
Pittsburgh, PA 15238
Visit our website at www.dorrancebookstore.com

ISBN: **978-1-6376-4077-7**
eISBN: **978-1-6376-4920-6**

BROKEN GLASS AND GASOLINE

CRASH

I am a social animal
Living in this brick mortar wood concrete cage of your design
You have slain my ambition
Driven my love to the sea
And drowned my sorrows
I am left a shell
Just trudging through the derelict life
Of a stranger's who I must now become
Who is this?
Why did I get cast in this part?
I want a refund for the ride
I don't want to play by these rules
I didn't order this
So much is left up to others
Must we be Thoreau to be free?
Life on the sails
Where the wind blows is where I can travel
Get my power from the sun
My sustenance from the sea
Alone on an ocean I can be me
Free from ignorance
My own that is
Just my guitar and the storms that mother throws at me
I can stick to coastal waters
I can travel the rivers
Visit the lakes
Or brave the oceans blue
Blue and deep and dangerous where true adventure lies
Where there are none but those I bring along
Live free and die alone

I SPEAK SO THE DEAD MAY BE HEARD

I speak for my death existentially and real.
I eulogize myself for the deaths I have already suffered.
Living every dream but the one that haunts.
Loving what's approved and shotgunning those desires
Deepest, dearest and most revolutionary
To the stained plaid that infested your childhoods.

Where is the fire that was burning?
Where is your opus written young, free, and under the stars?
Lost to the endless routine of alarm clocks and mileage,
Traffic jams and groceries - dentist appointments and family dinner.
That ember still smolders suffering softly under layers of comfort
And denial of a life properly conducted - but a proper life
Conducts no energy from sparks of irrational and abandoned genius.

I speak for the untold dead waking every morning
Sunrise defeating their eternal sleep for moments
Traded for false hopes and false dreams to nonexistent profits.
I watched the dream die in a field ripe for the harvest
As starving pickers plucked rotten fruits to sate their hunger to no avail.

Where is the vehicle of my ascendency - the stairway with golden rails?
What price is there to purchase a dead dream perpetuated by dogma?
Fortune favors the fortunate in endless firefly-like displays of masochistic
courtship rituals
Of a standard we collectively chose not to bear.
Still we cling to old patterns as we give lip service to a newborn secular
god state.

I am the dead man walking daily through my unused motivations,
Cold in heart but not cold hearted, my blood frosted by demands I never agreed to.
Circumstance is king and apathetic disregard the queen - careful, she moves in all directions,
But the king is silent and sneaking moving ever closer one box and then another at every turn.
The loveless shall inherit the Earth as we all lose our claim.

TOMORROW IS MY YESTERDAY

I'm a fucking time traveler
Your tomorrow is my yesterday
I know how it turns out
I know if you made the shot
Got the job
Rekindled love
Walked away from someone
Lived
Died
Gave up.

I know your coming daybreak stories
Your experience is my memory
I remember how you will
Stub that toe
Kill that man
Make love so passionately
Eat the last donut
Rat out your annoying coworker.

Your midnight confessions are
Yesterday's snooze for me
I already smelled that dirty laundry
Heard your Hail Marys
Did shots saying screw the bitch
Reminded you I own a shovel
Stopped myself and broke the cycle.

OCTOBER REVELATION

A cold October night brought me happiness
And indecision
And a feeling of loss
Indescribable until I understood that
The ends were justifiable.

The morning brought me a clarity of tears and
Sadness
That the night before kept away from me
Due to a gift that was given to me
From a familiar stranger that deprived me of desire.

Total passion for the eternity of my life.

Forever with and always without the truth comes inside
And tells me the truth of my inner nation.

ACCENSAMQUE

Maxime pulchra puella
In corde meo non ignite
Passio autem est vita
Et universum est scriptor

Vas implere
Beneficium accipere manibus meis
Passio enim est flamma
Beneficium accipere munusculum de manibus meis

A REPLY

To valley distant move I may,
If do these things you will, you say,
And if I find myself so bold,
Would you cherish, hand and hold?

While wool keeps warm on starry night,
Linen and silk are a wonderful sight,
And while perfumes do sweeten my air,
I much prefer roses and flowers fair.

A life of work yet full of love,
Am I a hawk and not a dove?
I accept your buckle, clasp and stud,
But I'll not touch coal nor mud.

Your vision does for me entice,
But I do worry to live on rice,
If so powerful a man you are,
You may take my love, just pack my car.

STROLL THE NEIGHBORHOOD

Walking on the sun
Caught inside a solar flare
My feet they try to run
There's nowhere left to go
I'm caught inside your solar mud

Climbing to the moon
It's been so long, how are you?
I see not much has changed
You are such a two-faced body
Face of Janus, that is - I'm so sorry

Driving to the stars
Going out to "A" Centauri
Did I miss you there?
My rocket ship
Has run out of fuel

Falling down to earth I
Crashed so hard I know I'm dying
The world it starts to burn
Watch the matchsticks that built it all
Do their job in all their glory

It's the ocean left for me
Lose my mind and make me salty
I'll search the world so free
Fill my sails with unknown passion
Spin the globe in a whirlwind pattern

Flying thru space with destination unknown
I'm one with the sky when it's time to sigh
Now the seasons change and I must soldier
On from something far from over

PRIMO

Alone
At last
At stake
At least.

Acquired
Admonished
Available
Absorbed.

Absolutely
Advantageous
Aggravated
Aggressive.

SHE WAS

Forthright in the dark,
You move and I see your body sway.
Troublesome from the start,
You smile and my defenses wave.
Coy and restrained,
You hold and I don't turn away.
Lost and in the dark,
I see but I can't tell.
Loving life full of laughter,
You turn and show me the way.
Fumbling from the start,
I smile yet how can I be sure?
Reaching for me in the night,
It's done and the truth is there.

You were my favorite story to read,
With lessons engraved on the curves of your body,
And the things you told late night with your body.

ROUNDABOUT

When this is over
Find me out
All your precious dreams
On your roundabout
At the end of all things
You will find me there
Like an endless winter.

Find another way
To bring it down
It's all about the way it sounds
You never turn away
Your too proud
Take a moment in the now.

Lost another day to time
Eventually it all declines
Face the future
Forget the past
Take one minute and
Fall down.

THIS IS NOT

All along this avenue of emotion
Like a rollercoaster ride on a thunderstorm day
I'm always here when you need me.
Funny how you're only here when you need me.

TO ALL A SAILOR S END

The storms and sea they call
As dangerous as danger be
No port of call no silent night
A well-trimmed course with rain swept sight.

A wave so rogue full force and proud
Tears the sail across the bow
Tiller lashed to waning hope
Rudder rests on failing rope.

Zeus almighty makes his presence known
Poseidon waits in the deep unknown
Break these clouds to the blue of day
For squall nor deep keeps sailors true at bay.

Travel on towards endless horizon
The sheet has flown - sails are jibing
Patience gone with anxious breath
Realize now all journeys end in death.

ROAR AND NEVER TIRE

I watch as passionate minds of similar creation to mine
Cry, drag, hurt, and heal through the streets
Of a dying dream.
I sit, bewildered and lost in a haze of disbelief.
Betrayed by an aristocracy that never was.
Denied by a class with no room left for my face.
Gather, gather a gathering gloom
Hashtag and pose give the SEO space to flow.
Fourteen nights then fourteen more
We wait for a solidarity that can never come.
Like a lost but still yearned for ex we can fake it
In the same room but really we want to either
Fuck or kill each other and nothing in between.
Talk your mess, they'll talk theirs, escalation is the
Nome de la terre.
Action begets action begets violence without hate
Without face, without a name except the ones the
Talking heads repeat over and over again
Just in case we missed it.
Just in case we opt to not kill each other like the animals
We are, we are made to be, we almost avoided but got
Tricked back into, that primal hating form.
There's no sense to your violence, no stress to your
Action, no loss to your senses.
Desensitized to the bullshit and no one cares.
Just causes usurped - did you catch that?
Just desserts - sorry, I'm on a diet
Strictly enforced by my Insta
Can't fall off this paleo - or is it keto today? -
Been counting carbs since 1992 and no one gives

A real fuck. Just swipe right if you got the looks and the
Dollars. There's no Springsteens anymore. Not enough
Shiny on those stained jeans that were ripped on a
Construction site not in a red sweatshop so they go for a hundred
But barely cost a damn dime.

Like mannequins, god damn idolatry we were warned but
It ain't cool to bend your knee at that particular altar no more.
Not that I'm one to gripe, I lost faith in the mystery behind the stars
When I realized anyone fucked up enough to let this shit
Happen is either not there or a prick, and anyway
I didn't vote for him or his kid.
I watch as the idiots and the profane become realized,
Actualized in a chamber of self-design where self-worth
Is all that matters and truth, well, that lady is not a pure thing.
What is your truth? - future epochs will look at this phrase to
Explain away the inexplicable barnacle we will become
On the roll call of human history.
A people is more important than a person, I is less than we,
And you are not us because we are not you.
You will never understand - origin points define the generation,
Only we know the real truth! Our truth, my personal truth that
Happens to be the same as yours and his and hers and zims and zers.
Dangerously close to a crowd of individuals - step back in line son,
That kind of thinking could get you doxed or make you internet famous.
Maybe those ripped jeans are online, music is heaving a dying breath.
Times, they be a changing...
Freedom isn't free, its 10.99 plus tax and a lifetime of lost sanity.
Sippin' on our struggleccino, everyone trying to claim that their
Drink is more bitter than the rest. They sell cream and sugar at the
Grocery store. Me, I'm an oat milk kinda guy, even I bow to a trend
On occasion. And no sugar in my damn coffee, I like mine strong,
A slap in the face like the first time you have to sleep on the cold hard

Ground and realize that home is a thousand miles away. That you
Left and you don't have a home anymore. A vagabond feather floating
On the gusts that come in off the ocean tide. Maybe you're flotsam, maybe
You're jetsam, maybe nobody gives a fuck.

I sit and watch. And mesmerize. And cry. And make plans to
Pull a Thoreau that I know deep down inside I will never follow through on.
I can't help it – it's like the morbid curiosity of a suicide jumper
In Manhattan drawing a crowd, and listening to the animals
Chant "Jump Jump Jump," just for street theater. A person passes by
At 120 mph and no one cares unless they get some on their shoes.
Check the tags, they're designer I see. No other way you're walking
Past like there's nothing to see. Speeding humans all downward bound.
I know you'll pray to an empty god and proselytize publicly at
Your digital altar. No quiet family donation, no spending time
At the shelter or the center. The blind cannot see the good deeds done
So why commit? Better to shine a light on it, make sure to take a look see
And share with friends than lift a single damned muscle to actually
Make something happen.
That is so last year.
IS this it, then? Do we get a choice or do we just roll with it, this
Compiled mess of existence that we have created.
La Belle Melange. Ring that fucking bell already, this round
Needs to be over. I guess we're going the full fifteen but
I don't know if I can make it - am I fighting Mike?
How many soundbytes does it take to get to the meat?
Oh, and its vegan substitute.
Take a bite and like it, smile into the camera everything will be okay.

I have to lie down; it is beyond measure. I crane my neck and still
I cannot see the ends of this eternity. Endless miasma of information,
Commentary, and opinion. Where is my lady I was looking for?
The only girl in town will be carrying scales. No sword, she's packing

Heat; welcome to tomorrow, after all. Maybe we should all be
Pagans again. Athena, Athena come back to us. You bring us war but
Also, with it wisdom. Your aspects are called upon - courage, valour, justice.
Our idols are false, and so are the temples. We need to rediscover some
ancient truths.
A universal human lore that will speak to us but not for us.
We have enough of that crap now. Jokers take charge and think they know
What the 'I's need and want but I hear a lot of we and us in that fucking
speech there.
Don't talk to me about some fucking esoteric greater good
When you can take care of simple, local good right here over and over instead.
I like to think of it as a hundred ones, not one hundred.

I wait and watch as a thousand sons line the streets, and a thousand daughters
Raise their voices. I wait for that final moment where we have made our choice
And all will tumble down a final path towards our doom, our destiny, our end.
To what end will it be?
What song will we sing together, arms linked and filled with a divine joy that
The day is won and we have love and understanding?
What knife will you choose should it go the other way?

EVACUATION

Just look.
Things were there all along.
Blessings.
And the unblessed too.
Sometimes we can tell the difference.
Occasionally we avoid joy.
I guess everyone is a little masochistic sometimes.

EXTINGUISHED

How often have I recollected your face,
the curves of your body, and the brush of your lips against my flesh?
Even now thoughts invade my mind of sweat,
bittersweet callings of my name on your lips and more on mine.

We sang our bodies as one, electric, morphing, transitioned
into a single spirit of sex and drive.
How often did we prey at each other's altar
only to become heretic - run afoul of our collective dogma and doctrine.
We are the money lenders Jesus ran from the temple.

Exchanges measured in fierce passion now gone cold.
Our currency now worthless.

No stoking the flames which would once melt the sun.
Only cold cranking oblivion for the engines that pumped fire through veins.
In endless expanse of linen I seek out your flame, that
blazing embrace which drove purpose home time and again.

You are the sun wild and irrepressible.
I live now only by starlight and moon.
What caravans do you wander now, I wonder?
What treasures have you discovered more valuable than our daily rhythms?

I reach out - it is not your unquenchable thirst I discover.
I am Apollo brought to deal with lesser nymphs in the unknown wilds.
There - with souls meek and eyes wide without depth - satisfiers cannot imagine
the strength and force and power derived from conjoined singularity.

Where is the place of concentration - is the path to it
lost amidst these barren fields?
Valleys that once gave fruit so succulent that
the gods fought for barely a taste?

If I were to find it, would I find you along the way?
Would you be there, waiting?
Would I even make the journey?
Who ever does?

LILY IN THE TIGER

I see you walking through the city
as I sit and consume my cup,
As a mist shrouds your body
I avoid death as I lose sight of your face.
With an over-large flower on your ear
and strength in your hand
your eyes are diamond - flawless, hard, beautiful.

With your long dress and your boots
the earth trembles as you pass,
awed by beauty, terrified by passion
and mesmerized by mystery.
This is the thief of my heart,
the beacon of my journey, the source
of all of my madness.

Unparalleled Aphrodite with
Athena in her heart,
Silver and gold adorn you and yet
Hold no sway over your soul.
Like Venus rising your radiance
shakes the very sky and cause him
and all his stars to fall as jewels
to be offered up to you.

THE SNOWFLAKE AND THE TEARDROP

What do we know of ourselves
that we do not know of others?
What can we say of ourselves
that we cannot say of others?
Like the intricate lattice work of newly falling snow
each of us is a creation of self left to land
where we may on this cold Earth
we all call home.
How different our unique selves
when we are all the same in difference?
We are all of us born of flesh, consumed by
the passions of existence
and returned to origin as our liquid selves -
formless held together by tensions,
tensions that run deeper than the surface
we offer the world.

Like a teardrop, salty and running, leaving its mark on a face it will never know.

TO THE SEA

to the sea
to ride the waves
to see the world
a life unheralded
the close of battle
the sun has set
to find the solace offered by the tides
and the crashing of the waves on the shore

the tide breaks
the ocean calls back
her own dominion
and seashells
crust my hand
as I lay here, tired and wanting,
grasping at the final rays of sunlight
before the moonrise comes and returns the tide

HEROINE GIRL

Your eyes are bright,
And you're always stealing.
Your beautiful smile,
And your evil ways.

Your eyes are bright,
And your hair's on fire.
You get what you want
Any way you can.

Yes, I will get your sin.

A Sea of green
High tide with deception.
The Height of heaven
But where's the gold now?

Your angel's wings
Crumbling down now.
The ladder's arms are
Too weak to hold.

What are these holes in your skin?

Your eyes aren't bright,
But you're still stealing.
You never smile,
And you kept your evil ways.

Your eyes are dull,
And your hair is knotted.
You get what you want
Any way you can.

Mother doesn't want you,
No.
Mother doesn't need you,
No.
You're always lying and stealing.
Yes.
You're my little girl.
You're my little Heroine Girl.

COME ALONG

I should come along to where my emotions are
but I don't go there anymore,
not since you smashed the lights and didn't pay the bill
and left me footing it to cover our expenses.

I will, eventually, but who can bear the burden left
of shattered mirrors? The shards crunch like eggshells
beneath my bare feet like some icon in an action movie,
but the only happy ending I get is on a table.

I grasped an angel that lights the beacon now,
fervent; like the fires burning prior to the burst
of a newborn star. From Freyr to Thor, she displays
particulars of a divine wildflower, blossoming in her own time.

Messengers provide, but no news can quench my thirst
or my desire. I suffer Tantalus' fate while my deeds would
Eleos take gratefully at his altar. Ancient gods, long bereft
of power, passion, and purpose. It's no wonder they come to mind.

Whatever chalk line or tied bits of strings that marked my way
long since had been replaced with trust. Bonds of truth are
stronger than what a fierce rain can wash away but are
steadfast when impassioned oaths are forgotten.
Within these mental catacombs I lose my direction.

MEDICINE MAN

I know what is real
And I know what I feel
I don't hate
I don't love
I don't know enough

I'll stay lost
I won't be found
I'll always seek untamed ground
I won't choose this or that
There's enough I'm where I'm at

Wake up young man
What's your story today?
They say you killed the species
Cause you liked it that way

Please don't explain
No one cares to hear
Your reasons are just lies
In the name of their fear

Can't excuse your demons
Its wings are too big to fold
Doesn't matter that they're
Shadows from a long time ago

You're the final losing chapter
You're the hand of fate
Your one of 50 million
But you all are the same

Told to feel sorry
Encouraged to not deserve
You're life's golden sunrise
But you're a child of dirt

TO MY ELUSIVE LOVER,

If I had time for your games,
I might enjoy them for a while.
We could sit on the riverbank
and imagine famous places
and stare into each other's faces
while I bring you gifts and sing your praises.

You could sit rapt yet resistant
withhold your love until hell freezes.
This would be appealing and
make my ardor grow.
A hundred perfect words for your eyes
and two hundred for each breast.
A novel for your body and the
whole collection for your heart.
You deserve this devotion
and I would gladly give you this purest love.

We grow no younger and time stops for no one.
The future lies before us
and life can pass us by should we not grasp it full.
Do not allow our love, pure, and untried,
to be kept for keeping's sake.
We all shall have ourselves alone
for company in the grave,
and only eternity as guest.
Let me sing your praises with more
than the words of my mouth before that final peace.

While glowing youth envelopes your flesh,
and your body warms from passion's blaze,
let us play a new game and pray at each other's heat.
Let us live exalted in each other's prowess,
not be tame to show our love.
We could pour our energy into that moment
and pull pleasure from this mundane life.
We cannot stop time, but we can dwell on our moments together.

TOMORROW AGAIN

I am a time traveler
Always travelling
No rest for the eternal
I am a time traveler
Constantly slipping tripping
Always moving forward
Time and space
Are my guardians
My allies
My lost confrontation.

I move amidst the stars
The planets, sun, the moon
The sky, the Earth, the ocean
And death
There is no
Final destination
There is no end of this journey
Everything continues on
Until it does not.

TAKE THIS, THINGS A DEMON TOLD ME

Unto thine own selfishness be true.
To your own wants, needs and desires - be true.
Forever chase after what you hold dear and never falter - never steer clear of your goals, hopes and aspirations.

Take.

Forever focus in visuals - do not be distracted by the word.
Hold tightly to that which makes your blood burn and avoid the consolation of those who have not accomplished.
Sleep late and rise early.
Do not avoid sin for it will drive you.
Early graves are a luxury for those who burn candles at both ends.

Take.

Do not trouble yourself with words of bonds and manipulate your situation for your own truths.
Ignore the plight of others and go back on promises.
Lie for love only to get what you need and use them willingly and wantonly.
We will all be in our graves before long so what does it matter?

Take.

What life of love and erudition could compare?
Holding back from desire will only serve to impair the burning passions that guide you.
Sell yourself, sell others and sell the world.

The future is now, don't hold back!
Press the advantage while your partner falters in theirs!

Take.

Remember the first rule - truth to your selfishness!
Time is short but never is it too late to rise above.
That which does not make you poorer makes you stronger.
Eat the cake, take a pill for the calories.

Take all that you crave.
Your want is paramount.
Self-gratification is key, tomorrow be damned.
Favors done in the past are meaningless in the now.
You owe nothing to anyone, and the world owes you everything.

Forever sleep.

THE SHORE

The shore
A mindless, body less thing
I love, for what it stands
Neither beginning nor end
Nor one or the other
But the shore.

I wish to live the shore
To have its wondrous bounty be my own
To have life upon life
And to feel the flowing nature
The movement of the tides and the love that causes
Beneath the crashing of water on sand.

Lives broken on the shore
The shore -hearts shattered
The shore – eyes denied
The shore – smiles turned upside down into frowns
I want to live on the shore
I make love on the shore.

Sometimes I want to make love to the shore
And feel the flow of the tide and rhythm
And the warm frozen embrace
Of forsaken mother earth
I take advantage of as I
Offer meager insults in the form of
A cigarette butt flying out to her cold waters.

Yet still I love the shore

Endless boundary – reach my hand out
And feel another world
The high tide coming faster
As the moon sheds a cloudy tear
That drips drips drips on Verrazano span
And separates all except for this
Mindless boundary I call the shore.

BOTTLE TALK B.S.

Half-full bottle of cream soda
Fills the table with a concept
I don't know.

One cigarette in the ashtray and
A pack of smokes on the table.
I reach out and light my cancer
With half closed eyes and
Let the smoke flow up my face
With a pointless conversation going.

Doesn't anyone respect the power of silence?

Does no one realize how much is said
Without words and the power of beauty?

Little, slowly flow until it's gone
And cast away the remnants
Only to be full again.

NIGHT DRIVE

Yellow line
Yellow line
Twisting into night
I follow you through darkness
Into unexpected light.

CPSIA information can be obtained
at www.ICGtesting.com
Printed in the USA
BVHW041026040821
613618BV00012B/171